Fairy Tale Theater
PETER PAN

Illustrations by: ROSER RIUS
Adapted by: MÓNICA BOSOM

CHARACTERS:
Narrator, Peter Pan, Tinker Bell, Wendy, John, and Michael Darling, the Lost Boys, Captain Hook, the Pirates, the Crocodile

Narrator:

Many years ago, there lived in the city of London, England, a girl and her two brothers, Wendy, John, and Michael Darling. Every night, Wendy told her brothers stories about Peter Pan and the Lost Boys who lived in Neverland, where children never grow up. What Wendy did not know was that Peter Pan really existed and was about to come into their bedroom. Peter Pan was chasing his shadow and there was a very tiny fairy with him, called Tinker Bell.

Wendy:

"What is that noise? Oh, you are Peter Pan! But what are you doing, separated from your shadow? Come over here and I will sew it to your feet so it will not go away again."

Peter Pan: *(Checking that his shadow is well sewed)*

"Wendy, come with me to Neverland and you can tell stories to the Lost Boys and be their mother."

John and Michael:

"Oh, yes, come on, Wendy, let's go. And can we fight the Pirates?"

Peter Pan:

"You can fight the Indians and the Pirates, and you will see mermaids and the faces of the trees..."

Wendy, John, and Michael:

"Yes, we will come with you! But wait—we can't fly..."

Peter Pan:

"Nothing easier: Just think wonderful thoughts, and with a little fairy powder, flying is the easiest thing in the world. *(Tinker Bell sprinkles sparkling dust over the three children.)* Follow me, the address is second star to the right and straight until morning."

Narrator:

The three children, Peter Pan, and Tinker Bell fly over the roofs of the city and they do not stop until the sun opens its eyes to start a new day. From high above in the sky they can see an island where there is an Indian camp and a pirate ship circling the island.

Peter Pan:

"That is Captain Hook's ship. Some time ago a Crocodile bit off his hand, including his watch, and now the watch goes tick-tock in its belly. The Crocodile vowed that one day it would eat up the Captain himself."

Narrator:

Meanwhile, the fairy is the first to arrive. She is jealous of Wendy.

Tinker Bell: *(Talking to the Lost Boys)*

"Can you see that bird coming toward us? *(pointing to Wendy)* Shoot your arrows at it—it is dangerous!"

The Lost Boys: *(They shoot their arrows.)*
"Tinker Bell, it looks like we have hit it!"

Peter Pan: *(Comes down fast to help the girl)*
"What happened? Is she dead? Oh! It's a good thing the arrow hit a button."

The Lost Boys:
"Tinker Bell told us to shoot our arrows."

Peter Pan:

"You are mean, Tinker Bell. I will not talk to you for a week!"

Narrator:

The Lost Boys live in an underground house to be safe from the Indians, who were always after them. One day, Peter Pan saves the Indian princess from being captured by Captain Hook. The Indians are so grateful that they stop chasing the children and they all become friends.

(Inside the ship that circles the island)

Captain Hook:

"Men, listen to me. We have to kidnap the children and demand a ransom."

Pirates:

"That is a fine plan, Captain Hook, but how can we do it?"

Captain Hook:

"We will wear costumes to look like Indians and stand in front of the underground house. Then we will call the children and capture them as they come out."

Pirates:

"Good, that is what we will do. And what will you do, Captain?"

Captain Hook:

"I will wait until Peter Pan is asleep and I will pour this poison in his glass of water. Ha, ha, ha!!!"
(He laughs in an evil way.)

Narrator:

In a little while, all the children have been captured and Peter Pan's glass of water has been poisoned.

Peter Pan: *(When he wakes up, he is thirsty and pours some water.)*

"This nap has made me thirsty."

Narrator:

Tinker Bell had seen that the Captain had poisoned the water. She takes the glass away from Peter Pan and drinks up the water to save him.

Peter Pan:
    "Tinker Bell, what is wrong? She is dying!"

Tinker Bell:
    "I am so sleepy..."

Peter Pan:

"This is Captain Hook's doing. I know—if all the children clap their hands, Tinker Bell will be saved. *(He shouts.)* Children of the world, if you believe in fairies, clap your hands very loud!" *(Great clapping is heard and the fairy recovers.)*

Tinker Bell:

"Thank you, Peter Pan. Now let's go rescue the children."

Peter Pan:

"Let's go to the ship. I will try to distract Captain Hook while you free the children, Tinker Bell."

Narrator:

And they fly toward the ship. Peter Pan imitates the sound of the clock coming from the Crocodile that has always frightened Captain Hook: tick, tock, tick, tock...

Captain Hook:

"I know that sound! Find that horrible animal and kill it! *(He sees Peter Pan on top of the ship's mast.)* It's you, Peter Pan! Aha! You have fallen into my hands!"

Peter Pan:

"Free the children!"

Captain Hook:

"First you will have to fight with me and win."

Narrator:

Peter Pan and Captain Hook begin to fight as they run up and down the ship. Suddenly, Peter Pan looks down and sees the big open mouth of the Crocodile, patiently waiting for Captain Hook to fall.

Peter Pan: *(Captain Hook almost falls.)*

"Careful, Captain Hook. There's the Crocodile!"

Captain Hook:

"Do you think I am stupid? You cannot fool me so easily..."

Crocodile:

Tick, tock, tick, tock... *(Captain Hook turns around when he hears this noise, loses his balance, and falls into the great mouth of the Crocodile.)*

Peter Pan:

"I have won, Captain Hook!"

Tinker Bell:

"Peter Pan, the children are free
            and the Pirates are jumping into
                    the sea."

Peter Pan:

"Now the island will be in peace. We are free from the dangerous Pirates, the Indians will live peacefully, and all the children will be able to go back home."

Narrator:

Wendy, John, and Michael fly back to London.

Wendy:

"We are back home, but don't you think our parents will have noticed our absence, Peter?"

Peter Pan:

"Don't worry. For the rest of the world, it has been only one night, the same night you sewed my shadow, Wendy."

Narrator:

And this is how Peter Pan and Tinker Bell said good-bye to the three children, promising to come to visit them every year. While the three children wave their hands from the window, Peter Pan becomes lost in the distance, surrounded by the fairy dust that Tinker Bell sprinkles everywhere.

ACTIVITIES

Some of the activities related to this play can include:

1. Children can act out their answers to questions or their responses to certain situations in mime. Children may make gestures, without talking, that represent their responses, to some of the following:
   — What do they like about their home?
   — What do they like about their friends?
   — What do they like about their family?
   — What do they do when they are happy or sad?

2. Make a kite that can fly like Peter Pan. You will need some thin wooden sticks, wrapping paper, nylon thread, glue, and a piece of cardboard to keep the thread rolled up on. First make a cross with two of the wooden sticks by gluing them together. Connect the four ends of the cross with the remaining sticks by gluing them in place. Attach one end of the nylon thread to one of the kite's tips. Keep the remaining thread rolled around the piece of cardboard.

Glue the wrapping paper to the kite's frame. Finish by adding a tail made of smaller strips of wrapping paper to the other tip of the kite.

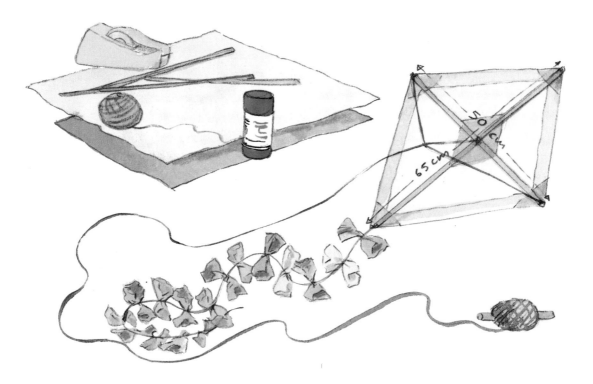

3. Make a hat like those worn by Tinker Bell, Peter Pan, or a Pirate. You will need some construction paper, colored pencils, glue, and a stapler. To make a hat like Peter Pan's or Tinker Bell's, form a cone using the construction paper and staple it in place. For a pirate hat, make a triangle with the construction paper. You can then decorate each hat with the colored pencils and smaller pieces of paper that can be glued in place.

4. Another activity consists of making very simple finger puppets. Cut out each character shown in the illustration and paste onto cardboard. Make the two cuts indicated in the drawing.

Place the puppets on your fingers and act out the story.

cut

cut

cut

cut

cut

cut

cut

cut

cut

cut

cut

cut

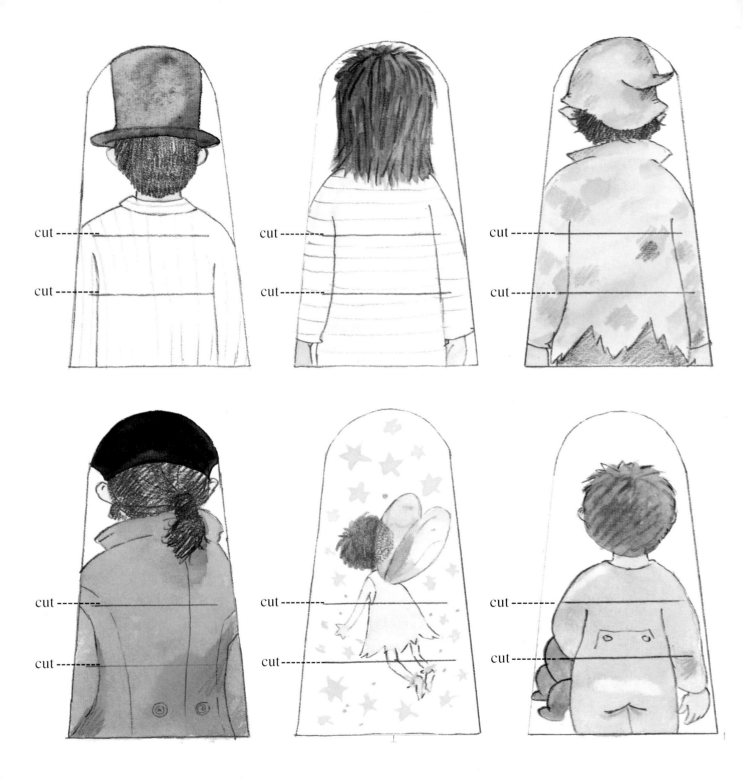

English language version published by Barron's Educational Series, Inc., 1999

Original title of the book in Catalan:
PETER PAN
One in the series *Teatre dels contes*
Illustrations by Roser Rius
Adapted by Mónica Bosom
Design by Carme Peris

All inquiries should be addressed to:
Barron's Educational Series, Inc.
250 Wireless Boulevard
Hauppauge, New York 11788
http://www.barronseduc.com

International Standard Book No. 0-7641-5153-3

Library of Congress Catalog Card No. 98-73629

Printed in Spain
9 8 7 6 5 4 3 2 1